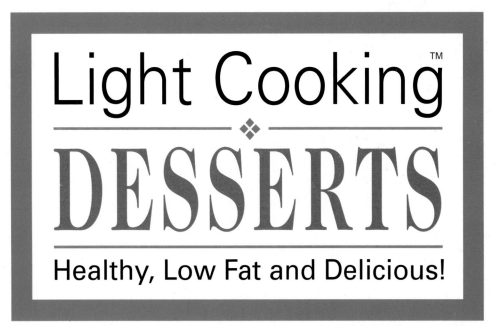

Light Cooking ™

DESSERTS

Healthy, Low Fat and Delicious!

PUBLICATIONS INTERNATIONAL, LTD.

Light Cooking is a trademark of Publications International, Ltd.

Food Guide Pyramid source: U.S. Department of Agriculture/U.S. Department of Health and Human Services.

Recipe Development: Jeanne Jones; Sue Spitler, Food Consultant, Incredible Edibles, Ltd.
Nutritional Analysis: Linda R. Yoakam, M.S., R.D.

Photography: Burke/Triolo Productions, Culver City, CA

Pictured on the front cover: Fruited Meringue Hearts Melba *(page 56)*.
Pictured on the inside front cover: Apricot Crumb Squares *(page 38)*.
Pictured on the inside back cover: Strawberry Cream Pie *(page 14)*.
Pictured on the back cover *(counterclockwise from top right):* Lemon Poppy Seed Cake *(page 82)*, Strawberry Crêpes Suzette *(page 49)*, Mocha Parfait *(page 54)* and Carrot Cake *(page 78)*.

ISBN: 0-7853-0794-X

Manufactured in U.S.A.

8 7 6 5 4 3 2 1

CONTENTS

LESSONS IN SMART EATING

Today, people everywhere are more aware than ever before about the importance of maintaining a healthful lifestyle. In addition to proper exercise, this includes eating foods that are lower in fat, sodium and cholesterol. The goal of *Light Cooking* is to provide today's cook with easy-to-prepare recipes that taste great, yet easily fit into your dietary goals. Eating well is a matter of making smarter choices about the foods you eat. Preparing the recipes in *Light Cooking* is your first step toward making smart choices a delicious reality.

A Balanced Diet

The U.S. Department of Agriculture and the Department of Health and Human Services have developed a Food Guide Pyramid to illustrate how easy it is to eat a healthier diet. It is not a rigid prescription, but rather a general guide that lets you choose a healthful diet that's right for you. It calls for eating a wide variety of foods to get the nutrients you need and, at the same time, the right amount of calories to maintain a healthy weight.

Food Guide Pyramid
A Guide to Daily Food Choices

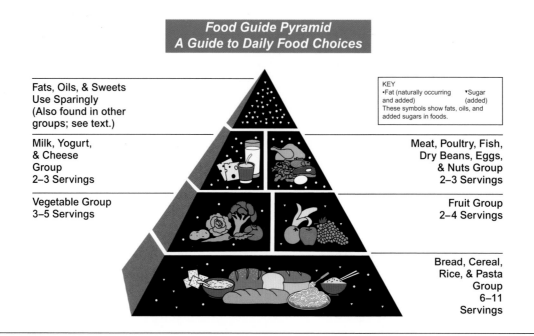

Fats, Oils, & Sweets
Use Sparingly
(Also found in other
groups; see text.)

KEY
•Fat (naturally occurring ▼Sugar
and added) (added)
These symbols show fats, oils, and
added sugars in foods.

Milk, Yogurt,
& Cheese
Group
2–3 Servings

Meat, Poultry, Fish,
Dry Beans, Eggs,
& Nuts Group
2–3 Servings

Vegetable Group
3–5 Servings

Fruit Group
2–4 Servings

Bread, Cereal,
Rice, & Pasta
Group
6–11
Servings

The number of servings, and consequently, the number of calories a person can eat each day, is determined by a number of factors, including age, weight, height, activity level and gender. Sedentary women and some older adults need about 1,600 calories each day. For most children, teenage girls, active women and many sedentary men 2,000 calories is about right. Teenage boys, active men and some very active women use about 2,800 calories each day. Use the chart below to determine how many servings you need for your calorie level.

Personalized Food Group Servings for Different Calorie Levels*			
	1,600	2,000	2,800
Bread Group Servings	6	8	11
Vegetable Group Servings	3	4	5
Fruit Group Servings	2	3	4
Milk Group Servings	2–3**	2–3**	2–3**
Meat Group Servings (ounces)	5	6	7

* Numbers may be rounded.
** Women who are pregnant or breast-feeding, teenagers and young adults to age 24 need 3 or more servings.

Lower Fat for Healthier Living

It is widely known that most Americans' diets are too high in fat. A low fat diet reduces your risk of getting certain diseases and helps you maintain a healthy weight. Studies have shown that eating more than the recommended amount of fat (especially saturated fat) is associated with increased blood cholesterol levels in some adults. A high blood cholesterol level is associated with increased risk for heart disease. A high fat diet may also increase your chances for obesity and some types of cancer.

Nutrition experts recommend diets that contain 30% or less of total daily calories from fat. The "30% calories from fat" goal applies to a total diet over time, not to a single food, serving of a recipe or meal. To find the approximate percentage of calories from fat use this easy 3-step process:

1 Multiply the grams of fat per serving by 9 (there are 9 calories in each gram of fat), to give you the number of calories from fat per serving.

2 Divide by the total number of calories per serving.

3 Multiply by 100%.

For example, imagine a 200 calorie sandwich that has 10 grams of fat.
To find the percentage of calories from fat, first multiply the grams of fat by 9:
$$10 \times 9 = 90$$

Then, divide by the total number of calories in a serving:
$$90 \div 200 = .45$$

Multiply by 100% to get the percentage of calories from fat:
$$.45 \times 100\% = 45\%$$

You may find doing all this math tiresome, so an easier way to keep track of the fat in your diet is to calculate the total *grams* of fat appropriate to your caloric intake, then keep a running count of fat grams over the course of a day. The Nutrition Reference Chart on page 92 lists recommended daily fat intakes based on calorie level.

Defining "Fat Free"

It is important to take the time to read food labels carefully. For example, you'll find many food products on the grocery store shelves making claims such as "97% fat free." This does not necessarily mean that 97% of the *calories* are free from fat (or that only 3 percent of calories come from fat). Often these numbers are calculated by weight. This means that out of 100 grams of this food, 3 grams are fat. Depending on what else is in the food, the percentage of calories from fat can be quite high. You may find that the percent of calories *from fat* can be as high as 50%.

Daily Values

Fat has become the focus of many diets and eating plans. This is because most Americans' diets are too high in fat. However, there are other important nutrients to be aware of, including saturated fat, sodium, cholesterol, protein, carbohydrates and several vitamins and minerals. Daily values for these nutrients have been established by the government and reflect current nutritional recommendations for a 2,000 calorie reference diet. They are appropriate for most adults and children (age 4 or older) and provide excellent guidelines for an overall healthy diet. The chart on page 92 gives the daily values for 11 different items.

Nutritional Analysis

Every recipe in *Light Cooking* is followed by a nutritional analysis block that lists certain nutrient values for a single serving.

■ The analysis of each recipe includes all the ingredients that are listed in that recipe, *except* ingredients labeled as "optional" or "for garnish."

■ If a range is given in the yield of a recipe ("Makes 6 to 8 servings" for example), the *lower* yield was used to calculate the per serving information.

■ If a range is offered for an ingredient ("¼ to ⅛ teaspoon" for example), the *first* amount given was used to calculate the nutrition information.

■ If an ingredient is presented with an option ("2 cups hot cooked rice or noodles" for example), the *first* item listed was used to calculate the nutritional information.

■ Foods shown in photographs on the same serving plate and offered as "serve with" suggestions at the end of a recipe are *not* included in the recipe analysis unless they are listed in the ingredient list.

■ Meat should be trimmed of all visible fat since this is reflected in the nutritional analysis.

■ In recipes calling for cooked rice or noodles, the analysis was based on rice or noodles that were prepared without added salt or fat unless otherwise mentioned in the recipe.

The nutrition information that appears with each recipe was calculated by an independent nutrition consulting firm. Every effort has been made to check the accuracy of these numbers. However, because numerous variables account for a wide range of values in certain foods, all analyses that appear in this book should be considered approximate.

The recipes in this publication are *not* intended as a medically therapeutic program, nor as a substitute for medically approved diet plans for people on fat, cholesterol or sodium restricted diets. You should consult your physician before beginning any diet plan. The recipes offered here can be a part of a healthy lifestyle that meets recognized dietary guidelines. A healthy lifestyle includes not only eating a balanced diet, but engaging in proper exercise as well.

All the ingredients called for in these recipes are generally available in large supermarkets, so there is no need to go to specialty or health food stores. You'll also see an ever-increasing amount of reduced fat and nonfat products available in local markets. Take advantage of these items to reduce your daily fat intake even more.

General Guidelines

■ Read the entire recipe before beginning to make sure you have all the necessary ingredients and baking utensils.

■ Measure all the ingredients accurately and assemble them in the order they are called for in the recipe.

■ Toast and chop nuts, and peel and slice fruit before preparing dough or batter.

■ Follow recipe directions and baking times exactly. Check for doneness using the test given in the recipe.

Storage Hints

After preparing these tasty treats, you will want to be sure they're stored properly.

■ Store cookies at room temperature in airtight containers with tight-fitting lids.

■ Cakes topped with cream cheese, whipped cream or meringue frostings can be stored covered in the refrigerator. Insert a few wooden picks into the frosting to prevent covering from touching the cake.

■ Cream or custard pies or ones topped with meringue can also be stored loosely covered in the refrigerator.

A Message from Jeanne Jones

It is not necessary to give up your favorite desserts just to maintain a healthy diet. The secret is to learn how to make lighter, healthier versions of the sweets you like best. The goal in creating tasty, satisfying desserts that fit into today's healthy lifestyle is to lower the overall fat content without losing the taste, texture or appearance associated with the original dish. Achieving this goal requires finding alternative low fat ingredients to use as substitutes for the fats usually called for in dessert recipes.

In baking, fats such as butter and oil act to produce a moist texture. Substituting unsweetened applesauce for most of the fat works well. Puréed prunes are also a great subsitute for fat in full-flavored cakes and muffins, and when used with chocolate and ginger, you don't even taste the prunes.

Fat and cholesterol levels can also be lowered by using two egg whites for each whole egg called for or by substituting a nonfat, cholesterol free egg substitute. Even custards can be made successfully with egg whites only.

The recipes that follow can help you make smart, healthy decisions about the desserts you prepare. By serving desserts that are low in calories, fat and cholesterol, you can truly enjoy your favorite part of the meal. And with the fantastic variety offered here, you don't have to sacrifice flavor or convenience. Start making irresistible, low fat treats that will both please and captivate your family and friends by using the recipes in this revolutionary cookbook!

Jeanne Jones
Internationally Syndicated Food Columnist

PIES & CHEESECAKES

GRASSHOPPER PIE

This beautiful pie is simple to make and simply delicious to eat.

2 cups graham cracker crumbs
4 tablespoons unsweetened cocoa powder
¼ cup margarine, melted
1 package (8 ounces) nonfat cream cheese
1 cup 1% low fat milk
2 tablespoons green creme de menthe liqueur
2 tablespoons white creme de cacao liqueur
1½ teaspoons vanilla
1 container (4 ounces) frozen nondairy whipped topping, thawed

1 Spray 9-inch pie pan with nonstick cooking spray. Combine cracker crumbs, cocoa and margarine in medium bowl. Press onto bottom and up side of prepared pie pan. Refrigerate.

2 Beat cream cheese in large bowl with electric mixer until fluffy. Gradually beat in milk until smooth. Stir in both liqueurs and vanilla. Fold in whipped topping. Chill 20 minutes or until cool but not set. Pour into chilled crust. Freeze 4 hours or until set. Garnish, if desired.

Makes 8 servings

Nutrients per Serving:

Calories	310
(31% of calories from fat)	
Total Fat	11 g
Saturated Fat	3 g
Cholesterol	<1 mg
Sodium	196 mg
Carbohydrate	28 g
Dietary Fiber	0 g
Protein	3 g
Calcium	23 mg
Iron	2 mg
Vitamin A	81 RE
Vitamin C	<1 mg

DIETARY EXCHANGES:
2 Starch/Bread, 2 Fat

Cook's Tip

This incredible pie uses liqueur for its unique minty flavor, but you may substitute 1 teaspoon mint extract and 1 teaspoon vanilla for the liqueur, if you desire.

STRAWBERRY CREAM PIE

❖

Feature this cool combination of low fat cream cheese and fresh strawberries at your next party.

❖

Nutrients per Serving:

Calories	220
(31% of calories from fat)	
Total Fat	7 g
Saturated Fat	2 g
Cholesterol	8 mg
Sodium	333 mg
Carbohydrate	31 g
Dietary Fiber	1 g
Protein	7 g
Calcium	181 mg
Iron	1 mg
Vitamin A	163 RE
Vitamin C	16 mg

DIETARY EXCHANGES:
2 Starch/Bread, 1½ Fat

1 cup plus 1½ teaspoons all-purpose flour, divided
¼ cup plus 1 teaspoon sugar, divided
¼ teaspoon salt
¼ cup cold margarine, cut into pieces
¾ teaspoon white or cider vinegar
3 tablespoons ice water, divided
6 ounces nonfat cream cheese
2 ounces Neufchâtel cheese
¼ cup vanilla nonfat yogurt
2 egg whites
½ teaspoon vanilla
1½ cups fresh strawberries, cut in half lengthwise
¼ cup strawberry jelly

1 Combine 1 cup flour, 1 teaspoon sugar and salt in medium bowl. Cut in margarine using 2 knives or pastry blender until small crumbs form. Add vinegar and 2 tablespoons ice water; stir until moist but slightly firm. If necessary, add remaining 1 tablespoon ice water. Gather dough into a ball.

2 Preheat oven to 450°F. Roll out dough into a 12-inch circle on lightly floured surface. Place dough in 9-inch glass pie pan. Bake 10 to 12 minutes or until lightly browned. Cool on wire rack. *Reduce oven temperature to 325°F.*

3 Combine cream cheese, Neufchâtel, remaining ¼ cup sugar and 1½ teaspoons flour in large bowl. Beat with electric mixer until creamy. Beat in yogurt, egg whites and vanilla; mix well. Pour cheese mixture into cooled pie crust. Bake 25 minutes or until set. Cool on wire rack.

4 Place strawberries on top of cooled pie. Melt jelly over low heat in small saucepan. Carefully brush glaze over strawberries, allowing glaze to run onto cheese. Refrigerate 3 hours or overnight.

Makes 8 servings

CHOCOLATE PIE

½ cup reduced fat biscuit mix
3 tablespoons unsweetened cocoa powder, sifted
1¼ cups sugar
2 tablespoons margarine, melted
1 whole egg
3 egg whites
1½ teaspoons vanilla

1 Preheat oven to 350°F. Spray 9-inch pie pan with nonstick cooking spray. Set aside.

2 Combine biscuit mix, cocoa and sugar in large bowl; mix well. Add margarine, egg, egg whites and vanilla; mix well. Pour mixture into prepared pan.

3 Bake 40 minutes or until knife inserted in center comes out clean. Garnish with powdered sugar, if desired.

Makes 8 servings

On a low fat diet, there's no need to deny yourself a chocolate treat. This pie is as rich as a candy bar—with only 18% of calories from fat!

Nutrients per Serving:

Calories	194
(18% of calories from fat)	
Total Fat	4 g
Saturated Fat	1 g
Cholesterol	27 mg
Sodium	177 mg
Carbohydrate	38 g
Dietary Fiber	0 g
Protein	3 g
Calcium	12 mg
Iron	1 mg
Vitamin A	47 RE
Vitamin C	0 mg

DIETARY EXCHANGES:
2 Starch/Bread, ½ Fat

Cook's Tip

Unsweetened cocoa powder is a great way to add rich chocolate flavor to your diet without all the extra fat and calories. One tablespoon of cocoa contains only a half gram of fat and is naturally very low in sodium and cholesterol free.

LEMON MERINGUE PIE

Serve this cholesterol-free pie as a refreshing finale to any meal.

1 cup graham cracker crumbs
¼ cup powdered sugar
2 tablespoons margarine, melted
1 tablespoon water
1½ cups granulated sugar, divided
⅓ cup cornstarch
1½ cups hot water
¼ cup cholesterol-free egg substitute
1½ teaspoons grated lemon peel
½ cup fresh lemon juice
3 egg whites
½ teaspoon vanilla
¼ teaspoon cream of tartar

1 Preheat oven to 375°F. Combine graham cracker crumbs and powdered sugar in small bowl. Stir in margarine and water; mix until crumbs are moistened. Press crumb mixture onto bottom and up side of 9-inch pie pan. Bake 6 to 9 minutes or until edges are golden brown. Cool on wire rack. *Reduce oven temperature to 350°F.*

2 Combine ½ cup granulated sugar and cornstarch in medium saucepan over low heat. Gradually stir in hot water until smooth. Add egg substitute. Bring to a boil, stirring constantly with wire whisk. Boil 1 minute. Remove from heat; stir in lemon peel and lemon juice. Pour hot filling into cooled crust.

3 Beat egg whites, vanilla and cream of tartar in large bowl until soft peaks form. Gradually add remaining 1 cup granulated sugar, beating until stiff peaks form. Spread meringue over filling, sealing carefully to edge of crust.

4 Bake 12 to 15 minutes or until meringue is golden brown. Cool to room temperature before serving.

Makes 8 servings

PUMPKIN CHEESECAKE

❖

Try this delicious low fat cheesecake as an alternative to your traditional pumpkin pie for Thanksgiving dinner.

❖

Nutrients per Serving:

Calories	121
(15% of calories from fat)	
Total Fat	2 g
Saturated Fat	0 g
Cholesterol	4 mg
Sodium	56 mg
Carbohydrate	22 g
Dietary Fiber	1 g
Protein	4 g
Calcium	89 mg
Iron	1 mg
Vitamin A	662 RE
Vitamin C	2 mg

DIETARY EXCHANGES:
1½ Starch/Bread, ½ Fat

⅓ cup graham cracker crumbs
1 can (16 ounces) solid pack pumpkin
2 cups low fat ricotta cheese
1 cup sugar
3 tablespoons all-purpose flour
1 tablespoon nonfat dry milk powder
1 tablespoon ground cinnamon
1 teaspoon ground allspice
1 egg white
¾ cup canned evaporated skim milk
1 tablespoon vegetable oil
1 tablespoon vanilla

1 Preheat oven to 400°F. Spray 9-inch springform pan with nonstick cooking spray. Add graham cracker crumbs; shake to coat pan evenly. Set aside.

2 Combine pumpkin and ricotta cheese in food processor or blender; process until smooth. Add sugar, flour, milk powder, cinnamon, allspice, egg white, evaporated skim milk, oil and vanilla; process until smooth.

3 Pour mixture into prepared pan. Bake 15 minutes. *Reduce oven temperature to 275°F;* bake 1 hour and 15 minutes. Turn off oven; leave cheesecake in oven with door closed 1 hour. Remove from oven; cool completely on wire rack. Remove springform pan side. Cover cheesecake with plastic wrap; refrigerate at least 4 hours or up to 2 days. Garnish with fresh fruit, if desired.

Makes 16 servings

LOW FAT CHEESECAKE

❖

This incredibly delicious cheesecake is so rich and creamy you won't believe that it's so low in fat!

❖

Nutrients per Serving:

Calories	266
(24% of calories from fat)	
Total Fat	7 g
Saturated Fat	3 g
Cholesterol	22 mg
Sodium	296 mg
Carbohydrate	39 g
Dietary Fiber	1 g
Protein	14 g
Calcium	191 mg
Iron	1 mg
Vitamin A	453 RE
Vitamin C	<1 mg

DIETARY EXCHANGES:
2 Starch/Bread, ½ Milk,
1½ Fat

1 cup whole grain bagel-shaped cereal
½ cup zwieback crumbs
1 cup plus 2 tablespoons sugar, divided
2 tablespoons water
2 teaspoons margarine, melted
3 cups nonfat ricotta cheese
1½ cups reduced fat cream cheese
1 cup low fat sour cream
2 egg whites
3 tablespoons cornstarch
1 tablespoon vanilla
1 teaspoon grated lemon peel
    Blueberry Sauce or Pineapple Sauce (page 24) (optional)

1 Preheat oven to 325°F. Spray 10-inch springform pan with nonstick cooking spray. Combine cereal, zwieback crumbs and 2 tablespoons sugar in food processor or blender; process until fine crumbs form. Gradually add water and margarine; process until moistened. Press crumb mixture onto bottom and up side of prepared pan. Set aside.

2 Place ricotta cheese in food processor or blender; process about 2 minutes or until smooth. Add cream cheese, remaining 1 cup sugar, sour cream, egg whites, cornstarch, vanilla and lemon peel; process until smooth. Pour batter into prepared crust.

3 Bake 1 hour or until center is almost set. Turn off oven; leave cheesecake in oven with door closed 30 minutes. Remove from oven; cool completely on wire rack. Remove springform pan side. Cover cheesecake with plastic wrap; refrigerate at least 4 hours or up to 2 days.

Makes 12 servings

(continued on page 24)

Low Fat Cheesecake, continued

BLUEBERRY SAUCE

6 tablespoons blueberry jam
2 tablespoons lemon juice
2 tablespoons water
2 teaspoons cornstarch
1 teaspoon grated lemon peel
1 cup fresh or frozen blueberries, thawed, drained

1 Heat jam and lemon juice in medium saucepan over low heat. Stir together water and cornstarch; add to jam mixture. Cook until slightly thickened; let cool. Stir in lemon peel and blueberries. Serve with cheesecake.   *Makes 12 servings*

PINEAPPLE SAUCE

1 can (8¼ ounces) crushed pineapple in juice, drained (reserve juice)
1½ tablespoons cornstarch
1 tablespoon sugar
2 tablespoons spiced rum or 1½ teaspoons rum extract
½ teaspoon grated lemon or lime peel

1 Combine reserved pineapple juice and cornstarch in small saucepan; stir in sugar. Heat over medium heat until slightly thickened. Stir in rum; cool. Stir in crushed pineapple and lemon peel. Serve with cheesecake.   *Makes 12 servings*

BOSTON CREAM PIE

❖

*What a remarkable trio—
light cake, pudding filling
and a sinfully rich chocolate
glaze!*

❖

½ package light yellow cake mix
⅛ teaspoon baking soda
⅔ cup water
2 egg whites
1½ teaspoons vanilla, divided
1 package (3⅜ ounces) sugar-free instant vanilla pudding mix
1⅓ cups skim milk
Chocolate Glaze (page 26)

1 Preheat oven to 350°F. Spray 9-inch round cake pan with nonstick cooking spray. Lightly coat with flour. Set aside.

2 Combine cake mix and baking soda in large bowl; mix well. Add water, egg whites and 1 teaspoon vanilla. Beat on low speed of electric mixer 30 seconds. Increase speed to medium; beat 2 minutes.

3 Pour batter into prepared pan. Bake 30 minutes or until cake pulls away from side of pan and springs back when touched lightly in center. Remove from oven. Cool 10 minutes on wire rack. Invert onto serving plate; cool completely.

4 Combine pudding mix, milk and remaining ½ teaspoon vanilla in medium bowl. Beat on low speed of electric mixer 2 minutes. Set aside.

5 Prepare Chocolate Glaze.

6 Cut cake in half horizontally; carefully remove top half of cake. Spread bottom half with pudding mixture. Replace top half; spoon Chocolate Glaze over top. Let stand until glaze hardens. Cut into wedges.

Makes 8 servings

(continued on page 26)

Nutrients per Serving:

includes Chocolate Glaze

Calories	241
(9% of calories from fat)	
Total Fat	2 g
Saturated Fat	1 g
Cholesterol	1 mg
Sodium	275 mg
Carbohydrate	51 g
Dietary Fiber	0 g
Protein	3 g
Calcium	100 mg
Iron	1 mg
Vitamin A	25 RE
Vitamin C	0 mg

DIETARY EXCHANGES:
3 Starch/Bread, ½ Fat

Boston Cream Pie, continued

CHOCOLATE GLAZE

⅔ cup powdered sugar
1 tablespoon unsweetened cocoa powder
1 tablespoon water
½ teaspoon vanilla

1 Sift together powdered sugar and cocoa in medium bowl. Add water and vanilla; mix well.

2 Add more water until desired spreading consistency.

❖

Cook's Tip
For a less rich dessert, try a dusting of powdered sugar instead of the chocolate glaze.

❖

THE CLASSICS

CHERRY COBBLER

The "cobbled" or bumpy appearance of the rich biscuit topping gives this favorite fruit dessert its unique name.

1 cup all-purpose flour
¾ cup sugar, divided
2 tablespoons instant nonfat dry milk powder
2 teaspoons baking powder
¼ teaspoon baking soda
¼ teaspoon salt
2 tablespoons vegetable oil
7 tablespoons buttermilk
2 tablespoons cornstarch
½ cup water
1 package (16 ounces) frozen unsweetened cherries, thawed and drained
½ teaspoon vanilla
   Nonfat frozen yogurt (optional)

1 Preheat oven to 400°F. Combine flour, ¼ cup sugar, milk powder, baking powder, baking soda and salt in medium bowl. Stir in oil until mixture becomes crumbly. Add buttermilk; stir until moistened. Set aside.

2 Combine cornstarch, remaining ½ cup sugar and water in medium saucepan. Stir until cornstarch is dissolved. Cook over medium heat, stirring constantly until thickened. Add cherries and vanilla; stir until cherries are completely coated. Pour into 8-inch square baking pan; spoon biscuit mixture over cherries.

3 Bake 25 minutes or until topping is golden brown. Serve warm with nonfat frozen yogurt, if desired.

Makes 8 servings

Nutrients per Serving:

Calories	204
(17% of calories from fat)	
Total Fat	4 g
Saturated Fat	1 g
Cholesterol	1 mg
Sodium	209 mg
Carbohydrate	40 g
Dietary Fiber	1 g
Protein	3 g
Calcium	53 mg
Iron	1 mg
Vitamin A	58 RE
Vitamin C	1 mg

DIETARY EXCHANGES:
2 Starch/Bread, ½ Fruit, ½ Fat

PEAR BROWN BETTY

❖

Hungry for something homey, warm and crunchy? Then this is the dessert for you. Pear Brown Betty features a spicy pear filling with a crunchy topping.

❖

Nutrients per Serving:

Calories	179
(17% of calories from fat)	
Total Fat	4 g
Saturated Fat	1 g
Cholesterol	0 mg
Sodium	40 mg
Carbohydrate	38 g
Dietary Fiber	3 g
Protein	2 g
Calcium	28 mg
Iron	1 mg
Vitamin A	37 RE
Vitamin C	5 mg

DIETARY EXCHANGES:
½ Starch/Bread, 2 Fruit,
½ Fat

8 medium pears, cored, peeled and sliced
¾ cup frozen unsweetened apple juice concentrate, thawed
½ cup golden raisins
¼ cup plus 3 tablespoons all-purpose flour, divided
1 teaspoon ground cinnamon
⅓ cup uncooked quick oats
3 tablespoons firmly packed dark brown sugar
3 tablespoons margarine, melted

1 Preheat oven to 375°F. Spray 11×17-inch baking dish with nonstick cooking spray. Set aside.

2 Combine sliced pears, apple juice concentrate, raisins, 3 tablespoons flour and cinnamon in large bowl; mix well. Spoon mixture into prepared baking dish.

3 Combine remaining ¼ cup flour, oats, brown sugar and margarine in medium bowl; mix until coarse crumbs form. Sprinkle evenly over pear mixture. Bake 1 hour or until golden brown. Cool in pan on wire rack. *Makes 12 (½-cup) servings*

❖

Health Note

Pears are a great source of copper, potassium, vitamin C, boron and fiber. You can find fresh pears beginning in late summer and continuing through winter.

❖

OLD-FASHIONED BREAD PUDDING

❖

The history of bread pudding dates back to the 1800's in England. Then it was eaten by the poor to make use of stale bread. Today we think of bread pudding as a rich treat.

❖

2 cups skim milk
4 egg whites
3 tablespoons sugar
2 tablespoons margarine, melted
1 tablespoon vanilla
2 teaspoons ground cinnamon
12 slices whole wheat bread, cut into ½-inch cubes
½ cup raisins
½ cup chopped dried apples

1 Preheat oven to 350°F. Spray 2-quart casserole with nonstick cooking spray. Set aside. Combine milk, egg whites, sugar, margarine, vanilla and cinnamon in large bowl; mix well. Add bread, raisins and dried apples. Allow to stand 5 minutes.

2 Pour mixture into prepared casserole dish. Bake 35 minutes or until well browned. Cool in pan on wire rack.

Makes 12 servings

Nutrients per Serving:

Calories	150
(19% of calories from fat)	
Total Fat	3 g
Saturated Fat	1 g
Cholesterol	1 mg
Sodium	214 mg
Carbohydrate	26 g
Dietary Fiber	1 g
Protein	6 g
Calcium	80 mg
Iron	1 mg
Vitamin A	48 RE
Vitamin C	1 mg

DIETARY EXCHANGES:
1 Starch/Bread, ½ Fruit, ½ Fat

❖

Cook's Tip

Be sure not to substitute another bread, such as white, for the whole wheat bread called for in this recipe. Various breads absorb pudding differently and substitutions may alter the amount of finished bread pudding.

❖

CARAMEL SUNDAE

1 cup 1% low fat milk
1 tablespoon cornstarch
1 tablespoon margarine
½ cup firmly packed dark brown sugar
1 teaspoon vanilla
1 pint vanilla ice milk or nonfat frozen yogurt, divided

1 Combine milk and cornstarch in heavy saucepan. Stir until cornstarch is completely dissolved. Add margarine and brown sugar; cook over medium-low heat, stirring constantly with wire whisk. Bring to a boil. Boil 1 minute. Remove from heat; stir in vanilla. Cool to room temperature.

2 Place ½ cup ice milk in each of four ice cream bowls. Top each with ¼ cup caramel sauce.

Makes 4 servings

What fun! In just minutes, you can add a sparkle to any day with this easy and tasty treat.

Nutrients per Serving:

Calories	262
(23% of calories from fat)	
Total Fat	7 g
Saturated Fat	3 g
Cholesterol	14 mg
Sodium	130 mg
Carbohydrate	47 g
Dietary Fiber	0 g
Protein	5 g
Calcium	191 mg
Iron	1 mg
Vitamin A	103 RE
Vitamin C	1 mg

DIETARY EXCHANGES:
3 Starch/Bread, 1 Fat

❖
Cook's Tip
Ice milk is made the same way as ice cream, except that it contains less butttermilk and milk solids. The result is a lower calorie count and a lighter texture.
❖

BROWNIES

❖

Moist and chocolaty, these cakelike brownies are sure to please the most devoted chocoholic.

❖

Nutrients per Serving:

Calories	81
(26% of calories from fat)	
Total Fat	2 g
Saturated Fat	<1
Cholesterol	0 mg
Sodium	37 mg
Carbohydrate	14 g
Dietary Fiber	0 g
Protein	1 g
Calcium	9 mg
Iron	0 mg
Vitamin A	0 RE
Vitamin C	0 mg

DIETARY EXCHANGES:
1 Starch/Bread, ½ Fat

½ cup boiling water
½ cup unsweetened cocoa powder
1¼ cups all-purpose flour
¾ cup granulated sugar
¾ cup firmly packed light brown sugar
1 teaspoon baking powder
¼ teaspoon salt
4 egg whites, lightly beaten
⅓ cup vegetable oil
1½ teaspoons vanilla
½ cup chopped unsalted mixed nuts (optional)

1 Preheat oven to 350°F.

2 Spray 13×9-inch baking pan with nonstick cooking spray. Combine boiling water and cocoa in large bowl. Mix until completely dissolved. Add flour, granulated sugar, brown sugar, baking powder, salt, egg whites, oil and vanilla; mix well. Fold in chopped nuts.

3 Pour mixture into prepared pan. Bake 25 minutes or until brownies spring back when lightly touched. Do not overbake. Cool in pan on wire rack; cut into squares.

Makes 32 brownies

❖

Cook's Tip

If you're short on light brown sugar, you may substitute granulated sugar, measure for measure. However, this may affect the color of the baked brownies.

❖

APRICOT CRUMB SQUARES

❖

Using a light packaged cake mix makes this delicious dessert not only healthy, but also easy to prepare.

❖

1 package (18.25 ounces) light yellow cake mix
1 teaspoon ground cinnamon
½ teaspoon ground nutmeg
6 tablespoons cold margarine, cut into pieces
¾ cup uncooked multigrain oatmeal cereal or quick oats
1 whole egg
2 egg whites
1 tablespoon water
1 jar (10 ounces) apricot fruit spread
2 tablespoons firmly packed light brown sugar

1 Preheat oven to 350°F. Combine cake mix, cinnamon and nutmeg in medium bowl. Cut in margarine with pastry blender or 2 knives until coarse crumbs form. Stir in cereal. Reserve 1 cup mixture. Mix egg, egg whites and water into remaining mixture.

2 Spread batter evenly in ungreased 13×9-inch baking pan; top with fruit spread. Sprinkle reserved 1 cup cereal mixture over fruit; top with brown sugar.

3 Bake 35 to 40 minutes or until top is golden brown. Cool in pan on wire rack; cut into squares.

Makes 15 servings

Nutrients per Serving:

Calories	267
(25% of calories from fat)	
Total Fat	7 g
Saturated Fat	2 g
Cholesterol	14 mg
Sodium	299 mg
Carbohydrate	48 g
Dietary Fiber	1 g
Protein	2 g
Calcium	59 mg
Iron	1 mg
Vitamin A	62 RE
Vitamin C	0 mg

DIETARY EXCHANGES:
3 Starch/Bread, 1½ Fat

❖

Health Note
Apricots are rich in beta-carotene, the substance that the body transforms into vitamin A, and are a good source of potassium.

❖

CARAMEL POPCORN

1 tablespoon margarine
1 cup firmly packed light brown sugar
¼ cup water
6 cups air-popped popcorn

1 Melt margarine in medium saucepan over medium heat. Add brown sugar and water; stir until sugar is dissolved. Bring to a boil; cover and cook 3 minutes.

2 Uncover pan; continue cooking mixture to the soft-crack stage (275°F on candy thermometer). *Do not overcook.* Pour hot mixture over popcorn; stir with wooden spoon.

3 Spread popcorn in single layer on sheet of aluminum foil to cool. When cool, break apart.

Makes 6 (1-cup) servings

❖

Nothing tastes better when watching your favorite movie than caramel popcorn. And you can feel better about snacking because it's so low in fat and calories.

❖

Nutrients per Serving:

Calories	195
(11% of calories from fat)	
Total Fat	2 g
Saturated Fat	0 g
Cholesterol	0 mg
Sodium	37 mg
Carbohydrate	44 g
Dietary Fiber	1 g
Protein	1 g
Calcium	33 mg
Iron	1 mg
Vitamin A	24 RE
Vitamin C	0 mg

DIETARY EXCHANGES:
2½ Starch/Bread, ½ Fat

❖

Cook's Tip

There are eight different candy stages. Each stage represents a different type of candy. For breakable caramel, the soft-crack stage (270°–290°F) on your candy thermometer is most effective.

❖

CRÈME CARAMEL

½ cup sugar, divided
1 tablespoon hot water
2 cups skim milk
⅛ teaspoon salt
½ cup cholesterol free egg substitute
½ teaspoon vanilla
⅛ teaspoon maple extract

1 Heat ¼ cup sugar in heavy saucepan over low heat, stirring constantly until melted and straw colored. Remove from heat; stir in water. Return to heat; stir 5 minutes until mixture is dark caramel color. Divide melted sugar evenly between 6 custard cups. Set aside.

2 Preheat oven to 350°F. Combine milk, remaining ¼ cup sugar and salt in medium bowl. Add egg substitute, vanilla and maple extract; mix well. Pour ½ cup mixture into each custard cup. Place cups in heavy pan and pour 1 to 2 inches hot water into pan.

3 Bake 40 to 45 minutes until knife inserted near edge of cup comes out clean. Cool on wire rack. Refrigerate 4 hours or overnight.

4 Before serving, run knife around edge of custard cup. Invert custard onto serving plate; remove cup.

Makes 6 servings

This wonderfully refreshing French dessert will cool your taste buds after a spicy main dish.

Nutrients per Serving	
Calories	103
(1% of calories from fat)	
Total Fat	<1 g
Saturated Fat	0 g
Cholesterol	1 mg
Sodium	114 mg
Carbohydrate	21 g
Dietary Fiber	0 g
Protein	5 g
Calcium	108 mg
Iron	0 mg
Vitamin A	153 RE
Vitamin C	1 mg

DIETARY EXCHANGES:
1 Starch/Bread, ½ Milk

SPECIAL OCCASIONS

CHOCOLATE MOUSSE

❖

This fabulous, nearly fat free mousse is lighter and airier than most chocolate desserts and is so quick and easy to make!

❖

½ cup plus 2 tablespoons sugar, divided
¼ cup unsweetened cocoa powder
1 envelope unflavored gelatin
2 tablespoons coffee-flavored liqueur
2 cups skim milk
¼ cup cholesterol free egg substitute
2 egg whites
⅛ teaspoon cream of tartar
½ cup reduced fat nondairy whipped topping

1 Combine ½ cup sugar, cocoa and gelatin in medium saucepan. Add coffee-flavored liqueur; let stand 2 minutes. Add milk; heat over medium heat. Stir until sugar and gelatin are dissolved. Stir in egg substitute. Set aside.

2 Beat egg whites in medium bowl with electric mixer until foamy; add cream of tartar. Beat until soft peaks form. Gradually beat in remaining 2 tablespoons sugar; continue beating until stiff peaks form.

3 Gently fold egg white mixture into cocoa mixture. Fold in whipped topping. Divide evenly between 8 dessert dishes. Refrigerate until thickened. Ganish, if desired.

Makes 8 servings

Nutrients per Serving:

Calories	118
(3% of calories from fat)	
Total Fat	<1 g
Saturated Fat	<1 g
Cholesterol	1 mg
Sodium	60 mg
Carbohydrate	23 g
Dietary Fiber	0 g
Protein	5 g
Calcium	83 mg
Iron	1 mg
Vitamin A	78 RE
Vitamin C	1 mg

DIETARY EXCHANGES:
1½ Starch/Bread

RASPBERRY TORTONI CAKE ROLL

You won't believe the compliments you'll receive with this extravagent-looking dessert! No need to tell them how easy it really was to prepare.

Raspberry Tortoni Filling (page 48)
3 eggs, separated
¾ cup granulated sugar
¼ cup skim milk
1 teaspoon vanilla
¾ cup all-purpose flour
1½ teaspoons baking powder
¼ teaspoon salt
¼ teaspoon cream of tartar
1 tablespoon powdered sugar
¼ cup fresh raspberries (optional)
Mint sprigs (optional)

1 Prepare Raspberry Tortoni Filling. Set aside.

2 Lightly grease 15×10×1-inch jelly-roll pan and line with waxed paper; lightly grease and flour paper. Preheat oven to 400°F. Beat egg yolks in medium bowl with electric mixer at high speed 1 minute; gradually beat in granulated sugar until yolks are thick and lemon colored, about 5 minutes. Beat in milk and vanilla; mix in flour, baking powder and salt.

3 With clean beaters, beat egg whites in medium bowl at high speed until foamy; add cream of tartar and beat until stiff peaks form. Fold about one-third egg white mixture into cake batter; gently fold cake batter into remaining egg white mixture. Spread batter evenly in prepared pan.

4 Bake 8 to 10 minutes or until cake begins to brown. Immediately invert onto clean towel that has been sprinkled with powdered sugar. Peel off waxed paper; roll cake up in towel and cool on wire rack only 10 minutes.

5 Gently unroll cake and spread with Raspberry Tortoni Filling. Roll cake up; wrap in plastic wrap or aluminum foil and freeze until firm, at least 8 hours or overnight.

6 Remove cake from freezer; unwrap and trim ends, if uneven. Place cake on serving plate. Garnish with additional powdered sugar, fresh raspberries and mint, if desired.

Makes 12 servings

(continued on page 48)

Raspberry Tortoni Cake Roll, continued

RASPBERRY TORTONI FILLING

2 cups fresh or frozen unsweetened raspberries, thawed, drained and divided
1 tablespoon sugar
2 envelopes (1.3 ounces each) whipped topping mix
1 cup 1% lowfat milk
½ teaspoon rum extract or sherry extract (optional)
¼ cup coarsely chopped pistachio nuts or blanched almonds

1 Place 1 cup raspberries in food processor or blender; process until smooth. Strain and discard seeds. Sprinkle sugar over remaining 1 cup raspberries.

2 Beat whipped topping mix with milk in medium bowl at high speed until stiff peaks form; fold in raspberry purée and rum extract, if desired. Fold in sugared raspberries and nuts.

Makes 4 cups

❖

Health Tip
Raspberries are a good source of fiber, potassium and vitamin C. They also contain a small amount of vitamin A and iron.

❖

STRAWBERRY CRÊPES SUZETTE

Nutrients per Serving:

Calories	94
(10% of calories from fat)	
Total Fat	1 g
Saturated Fat	0 g
Cholesterol	0 mg
Sodium	52 mg
Carbohydrate	17 g
Dietary Fiber	1 g
Protein	2 g
Calcium	35 mg
Iron	0 mg
Vitamin A	27 RE
Vitamin C	32 mg

DIETARY EXCHANGES:
½ Starch/Bread, ½ Fruit, ½ Fat

12 Crêpes (page 50)
 1 cup fresh orange juice
 2 teaspoons cornstarch
 2 tablespoons sugar
 2 teaspoons grated orange peel
 3 cups fresh strawberry slices
 ¼ cup orange-flavored liqueur
 1 teaspoon margarine

1 Prepare Crêpes. Set aside.

2 Combine orange juice and cornstarch in large saucepan. Stir until cornstarch is dissolved. Add sugar, grated orange peel and strawberries; mix well. Bring to a boil over medium heat. Reduce heat to low and simmer, stirring until slightly thickened. Remove from heat; stir in liqueur and margarine.

3 Arrange crêpes, folded in quarters, on serving dish. Spoon sauce evenly over top. Serve immediately. Garnish, if desired.

Makes 12 servings

(continued on page 50)

Strawberry Crêpes Suzette, continued

CRÊPES

1 cup skim milk
2 egg whites
½ cup whole-wheat flour
¼ cup all-purpose flour
1 tablespoon sugar
⅛ teaspoon salt
1½ teaspoons margarine

1 Combine milk, egg whites, both flours, sugar and salt in food processor or blender; process until well blended. Pour mixture into large bowl.

2 Melt margarine in nonstick crêpe or omelet pan over medium heat. Pour melted margarine into crêpe batter; mix well. Wipe pan with paper towel; save towel for later use. Heat pan over medium heat.

3 Spoon 2 tablespoons batter into hot pan; roll from side to side to cover entire pan surface. When edges of batter curl away from sides of pan, turn crêpe. Brown. Repeat with remaining batter; wipe pan with reserved paper towel between each crêpe. Keep crêpes warm in covered container until ready to use.   *Makes 12 crêpes*

❖

Cook's Tip
Choose fresh strawberries that are bright red and still have their green stems attached. Don't wash until ready to use. Store strawberries in a moistureproof container in the refrigerator for two to three days.

❖

LIME SURPRISE

This exceptionally flavorful treat is surprisingly simple to prepare!

2 whole eggs
6 egg whites
3 tablespoons margarine
1¼ cups sugar
1 tablespoon grated lime peel
¾ cup fresh lime juice
8 ounces lady fingers, divided

1 Combine eggs and egg whites in medium bowl; beat until foamy. Set aside. Combine margarine and sugar in top of double boiler. Melt margarine over simmering water. Add lime peel and lime juice; mix well.

2 Add egg mixture to margarine mixture; cook and stir until thickened, about 6 minutes. Remove from heat; cool completely.

3 Cut lady fingers in half lengthwise. Line bottom of 1½-quart soufflé dish or casserole dish with lady fingers. Cover with 1 cup of lime mixture. Continue layering until all lady fingers are used, ending with layer of lime mixture.

4 Cover tightly; refrigerate 6 hours or overnight. Garnish with grated lime peel, if desired.

Makes 12 (⅓-cup) servings

Nutrients per Serving:

Calories	200
(24% of calories from fat)	
Total Fat	5 g
Saturated Fat	1 g
Cholesterol	104 mg
Sodium	99 mg
Carbohydrate	34 g
Dietary Fiber	0 g
Protein	5 g
Calcium	17 mg
Iron	1 mg
Vitamin A	82 RE
Vitamin C	6 mg

DIETARY EXCHANGES:
2 Starch/Bread, 1 Fat

Health Note

New studies show that a naturally occurring chemical in citrus fruits, such as limes, may aid against certain forms of stomach cancer. Limes are also a good source of potassium and contain some vitamin C.

MOCHA PARFAIT

Mocha, the flavor combination of coffee and chocolate, is quickly becoming a favorite flavor for coffees, icings, desserts and sauces. Here we have made a low fat mocha sauce and poured it over nonfat frozen yogurt.

4½ teaspoons margarine
⅓ cup unsweetened cocoa powder
1 cup boiling water
½ cup sugar
1 tablespoon instant coffee granules
1 teaspoon vanilla
1 pint coffee-flavored nonfat frozen yogurt
12 whole coffee beans (optional)

1 Melt margarine in heavy saucepan over low heat. Add cocoa; cook and stir 3 minutes. Add boiling water, sugar and coffee; cook and stir until thickened. Remove from heat; stir in vanilla. Cool.

2 Place 2 tablespoons frozen yogurt in bottom of each of 4 parfait glasses. Top each with 1 tablespoon sauce. Top sauce with another 2 tablespoons frozen yogurt; top frozen yogurt with 2 tablespoons sauce. Repeat layering twice more. Top each parfait with 3 coffee beans, if desired.

Makes 4 servings

Nutrients per Serving:

Calories	265
(16% of calories from fat)	
Total Fat	5 g
Saturated Fat	1 g
Cholesterol	0 mg
Sodium	109 mg
Carbohydrate	54 g
Dietary Fiber	0 g
Protein	5 g
Calcium	15 mg
Iron	3 mg
Vitamin A	52 RE
Vitamin C	0 mg

DIETARY EXCHANGES:
3 Starch/Bread, 1 Fat

Cook's Tip

For caffeine-sensitive people, instant decaffinated coffee granules may be substituted for the regular granules. Store all instant coffee in an air-tight container in a cool place.

FRUITED MERINGUE HEARTS MELBA

❖

Show someone special how much you care by serving them this festive dessert!

❖

Nutrients per Serving:	
Calories	383
(0% of calories from fat)	
Total Fat	1 g
Saturated Fat	0 g
Cholesterol	0 mg
Sodium	60 mg
Carbohydrate	93 g
Dietary Fiber	8 g
Protein	5 g
Calcium	42 mg
Iron	1 mg
Vitamin A	109 RE
Vitamin C	55 mg

DIETARY EXCHANGES:
5 Fruit, ½ Lean Meat

6 egg whites
¼ teaspoon cream of tartar
¼ teaspoon ground allspice
1½ cups sugar
    Melba Sauce (page 58)
3 cups sliced assorted fruit (berries, melon, grapes)
    Mint sprigs (optional)

1 Line large cookie sheet with parchment paper; draw 6 hearts (3×3 inches) on paper.

2 Beat egg whites in large bowl with electric mixer until foamy. Add cream of tartar; beat until soft peaks form. Add allspice. Beat in sugar, 1 tablespoon at a time, beating at high speed until stiff peaks form, about 5 minutes.

3 Preheat oven to 250°F. Spoon meringue into large pastry bag fitted with medium star tip; pipe heart outlines on parchment paper. Fill in heart shapes with meringue. Then pipe second row on top of first row of meringue around outside edges of hearts to form rims.

4 Bake 1 hour or until meringues are firm and crisp to touch. Turn off oven; leave meringues in oven with door closed at least 2 hours.

5 Prepare Melba Sauce. Set aside. Fill meringue hearts with fruit. Spoon about ¼ cup sauce onto each dessert plate and place filled hearts on sauce. Garnish with mint sprig, if desired.

Makes 6 servings

(continued on page 58)

Fruited Meringue Hearts Melba, continued

MELBA SAUCE

   1 package (16 ounces) frozen unsweetened raspberries, thawed, drained
¼ cup sugar

1 Place raspberries and sugar in food processor or blender; process until smooth. Strain and discard seeds.

Makes 1½ cups

❖

Cook's Tip

The secret to successful meringue is properly beaten egg whites. For best results, follow these handy tips:

• Eggs are easier to separate when they're cold.

• Be careful not to get any egg yolk in the egg whites because this will prevent them from reaching fullest volume when beaten.

• Place egg whites in a glass or metal mixing bowl, not plastic.

❖

RASPBERRY NAPOLEON

This uniquely different, beautiful dessert is also very healthy. Raspberries are high in vitamin C and ricotta cheese is higher in calcium than any other cheese.

❖

Nutrients per Serving:

Calories	243
(15% of calories from fat)	
Total Fat	4 g
Saturated Fat	0 g
Cholesterol	21 mg
Sodium	18 mg
Carbohydrate	34 g
Dietary Fiber	3 g
Protein	19 g
Calcium	275 mg
Iron	1 mg
Vitamin A	209 RE
Vitamin C	16 mg

DIETARY EXCHANGES:
1 Starch/Bread,
2 Lean Meat, 1 Fruit

Butter-flavored nonstick cooking spray
4 sheets phyllo dough, divided
Napoleon Filling (page 60)
2 cups fresh or frozen raspberries, thawed, drained, divided

1 Preheat oven to 375°F. Spray cookie sheet with butter-flavored nonstick cooking spray. Set aside.

2 Place 1 sheet of phyllo on waxed paper. Cover remaining sheets with damp kitchen towel to prevent dough from drying out. Set aside. Spray phyllo with butter-flavored cooking spray. Cut phyllo into thirds lengthwise. Carefully fold 1 third in half; spray with cooking spray. Fold in half again; spray. Fold in half again forming rectangle; spray top with cooking spray. Place on prepared cookie sheet. Repeat folding and spraying with remaining 2 thirds.

3 Repeat step 2 with remaining phyllo dough.

4 Bake 7 to 9 minutes or until phyllo is golden brown. Cool on wire rack. Prepare Napoleon Filling.

5 Spread 2 tablespoons filling on each of 4 phyllo rectangles. Place, filling side up, on dessert plates. Top each with ¼ cup raspberries.

6 Spread 2 tablespoons Napoleon Filling on each of 4 more phyllo rectangles. Place, Filling side down, on top of raspberry layer. Spread top of each stack with 2 tablespoons Napoleon Filling. Top each with ¼ cup raspberries, reserving 4 raspberries for garnish.

7 Spread each of remaining 4 rectangles with 2 tablespoons Napoleon Filling. Place, filling side down, on raspberry layer. Top each stack with 1 tablespoon Napoleon Filling and 1 raspberry.

Makes 4 servings

(continued on page 60)

Raspberry Napoleon, continued

NAPOLEON FILLING

    1 container (15 ounces) low fat ricotta cheese
    1 container (15 ounces) nonfat ricotta cheese
    3 tablespoons sugar
    1 teaspoon vanilla
    ½ teaspoon lemon extract

1 Place both cheeses, sugar, vanilla and lemon extract in food processor or blender; process until smooth.

❖

Cook's Tip

When covering the phyllo dough with a damp kitchen towel, be sure the towel is only slightly damp. Otherwise, it will get the dough too wet.

❖

APPLE RAISIN RISOTTO

❖

If you like risotto for dinner, why not try it for dessert? This treat is similar to rice pudding, only with an imaginative twist.

❖

Nutrients per Serving:

Calories	218
(19% of calories from fat)	
Total Fat	5 g
Saturated Fat	1 g
Cholesterol	2 mg
Sodium	127 mg
Carbohydrate	38 g
Dietary Fiber	1 g
Protein	6 g
Calcium	191 mg
Iron	1 mg
Vitamin A	130 RE
Vitamin C	2 mg

DIETARY EXCHANGES:
½ Milk, 1 Starch/Bread,
1 Fruit, 1 Fat

3 tablespoons margarine, divided
1 large Golden Delicious apple, peeled, cored and diced
¾ cup arborio rice
⅓ cup raisins
¼ cup frozen unsweetened apple juice concentrate, thawed
1 cup unsweetened apple juice, divided
1 tablespoon firmly packed dark brown sugar
½ teaspoon ground cinnamon
1 can (12 ounces) evaporated skimmed milk
1½ cups skim milk
1½ teaspoons vanilla

1 Melt 2 tablespoons margarine in large, heavy saucepan over medium heat. Add apple. Cook and stir until apple can be easily pierced with fork. Add rice; stir until grains become shiny. Add raisins and apple juice concentrate. Cook and stir until all of concentrate is absorbed.

2 Add ½ cup apple juice. Cook and stir until most of juice is absorbed. Add remaining ½ cup apple juice. Cook and stir until most of juice is absorbed. Add brown sugar and cinnamon; mix well. Reduce heat to low.

3 Combine evaporated skimmed milk and skim milk in medium saucepan. Heat over medium heat just until mixture becomes warm. *Do not boil.* Remove from heat.

4 Add ½ cup milk mixture to rice mixture. Cook and stir until most of milk is absorbed; repeat until all milk mixture is used. Do not allow last addition of milk to be completely absorbed. Remove from heat. Stir in remaining 1 tablespoon margarine and vanilla. Garnish, if desired. Serve immediately. *Makes 8 (½-cup) servings*

FRESH FRUIT TRIFLE

❖

Originally from England, this healthy dessert consists of angel food cake doused with sherry, covered with custard and topped with an abundance of fresh fruits. A delightful way to have a serving of fruit a day.

❖

2 cups skim milk
2 tablespoons cornstarch
⅓ cup sugar
4 egg whites, lightly beaten
2 teaspoons vegetable oil
1½ teaspoons vanilla
6 tablespoons sherry or apple juice, divided
4 cups cubed angel food cake
6 cups diced assorted fruits (apricots, peaches, nectarines, plums and berries)

1 Combine milk and cornstarch in medium saucepan; stir until cornstarch is dissolved. Add sugar, egg whites and oil; mix well. Bring to a boil over medium-low heat, stirring constantly with wire whisk; boil until thickened. Remove from heat. Cool. Add vanilla and 2 tablespoons sherry.

2 Place one-third cake pieces in bottom of 2-quart glass bowl or trifle dish. Sprinkle with one-third remaining sherry. Spoon ⅔ cup custard over cake. Spoon one-third fruit over custard. Repeat process twice, ending with fruit. Serve immediately.

Makes 12 servings

Nutrients per Serving:

Calories	133
(8% of calories from fat)	
Total Fat	1 g
Saturated Fat	0 g
Cholesterol	1 mg
Sodium	111 mg
Carbohydrate	26 g
Dietary Fiber	2 g
Protein	4 g
Calcium	73 mg
Iron	0 mg
Vitamin A	89 RE
Vitamin C	9 mg

DIETARY EXCHANGES:
1 Starch/Bread, 1 Fruit

❖

Health Note

Recent studies have shown that people who eat more than two servings of fruit and vegetables a day are four times less likely to suffer from heart problems than people who eat less than one serving a day. Vitamin C, abundant in many fruits and vegetables, has also been found to reduce the risk of stroke and cancer as well as the risk of heart attack.

❖

CRANBERRY-APPLE STRUDEL

❖

Cranberries, with their slightly bitter taste, and apples, with their very sweet taste, work perfectly together in this marvelous strudel.

❖

Nutrients per Serving:

Calories	215
(20% of calories from fat)	
Total Fat	5 g
Saturated Fat	1 g
Cholesterol	0 mg
Sodium	118 mg
Carbohydrate	43 g
Dietary Fiber	2 g
Protein	2 g
Calcium	21 mg
Iron	1 mg
Vitamin A	20 RE
Vitamin C	4 mg

DIETARY EXCHANGES:
½ Starch/Bread, 2 Fruit,
1 Fat

Butter-flavored nonstick cooking spray
1 tablespoon margarine
1 tablespoon firmly packed light brown sugar
2 medium Golden Delicious apples, cored, peeled and diced
¼ cup raisins
1 can (16 ounces) whole-berry cranberry sauce
6 sheets frozen phyllo dough, thawed
3 tablespoons graham cracker crumbs, divided
¼ cup toasted almonds, chopped

1 Preheat oven to 375°F. Spray cookie sheet with butter-flavored nonstick cooking spray. Set aside. Melt margarine in large saucepan over medium heat. Add brown sugar, apples and raisins. Bring to a boil; reduce heat, cook 10 minutes or until apples can be easily pierced with fork. Remove from heat. Add cranberry sauce; mix well. Set aside.

2 Place 1 sheet of phyllo on piece of parchment paper with narrow side farthest away. Cover remaining sheets with damp kitchen towel to prevent dough from drying out. Spray phyllo with cooking spray; sprinkle ½ tablespoon graham cracker crumbs on phyllo. Overlap second sheet of phyllo over first sheet about 1 inch down from top. Spray with cooking spray; sprinkle with ½ tablespoon crumbs. Continue overlapping with remaining phyllo and crumbs, spraying with cooking spray between each layer.

3 Spoon cooled cranberry mixture into center of phyllo. Sprinkle chopped almonds over mixture. Fold bottom and sides of phyllo to cover mixture, forming an envelope. With floured hands, roll filled phyllo, jelly-roll fashion, to form strudel. Place strudel on prepared cookie sheet. Spray top with cooking spray. Make 8 diagonal cuts across top of strudel. Bake 12 to 15 minutes or until lightly browned.

4 Cool on wire rack 30 minutes. Cut crosswise into 8 pieces. *Makes 8 servings*

CAKES & COOKIES

ORANGE SOUR CREAM POUND CAKE WITH MANDARIN SAUCE

❖

In this time-honored recipe, sour cream provides the traditional rich flavor and smooth dense texture.

❖

Nutrients per Serving:

(cake with sauce)

Calories	260
(26% of calories from fat)	
Total Fat	8 g
Saturated Fat	1 g
Cholesterol	24 mg
Sodium	191 mg
Carbohydrate	44 g
Dietary Fiber	1 g
Protein	4 g
Calcium	47 mg
Iron	2 mg
Vitamin A	164 RE
Vitamin C	31 mg

DIETARY EXCHANGES:
2½ Starch/Bread, ½ Fruit, 1 Fat

6 tablespoons margarine, softened
1 cup sugar, divided
1 cup low fat sour cream
1 whole egg
2 egg whites
1 tablespoon frozen orange juice concentrate
1 tablespoon grated orange peel
2½ cups cake flour
½ teaspoon baking soda
¼ teaspoon salt
⅓ cup orange juice
Mandarin Sauce (page 70)

1 Preheat oven to 350°F. Grease and flour 9×5-inch loaf pan. Beat margarine in large bowl with electric mixer until fluffy; beat in ⅔ cup sugar. Beat in sour cream, whole egg, egg whites, orange juice concentrate and orange peel until smooth. Set aside.

2 Combine flour, baking soda and salt in medium bowl; add to margarine mixture. Beat at medium speed until smooth. Pour batter into prepared pan.

3 Bake 40 minutes or until cake is golden brown and wooden pick inserted in center comes out clean. Cool in pan on wire rack 5 minutes.

4 Bring orange juice and remaining ⅓ cup sugar to a boil in small saucepan. Remove from heat; cool slightly. Drizzle warm syrup over warm cake and let stand 10 minutes; remove cake from pan and cool on wire rack. Prepare Mandarin Sauce.

5 Serve cake slices with Mandarin Sauce.

Makes 12 servings

(continued on page 70)

Orange Sour Cream Pound Cake with Mandarin Sauce, continued

MANDARIN SAUCE

   1¼ cups orange juice, divided
     1 tablespoon cornstarch
     2 cans (11 ounces each) mandarin oranges, drained
     1 tablespoon honey

1 Bring 1 cup orange juice to a boil in small saucepan. Mix cornstarch and remaining ¼ cup orange juice in cup; stir into boiling juice. Boil until thickened, about 1 minute, stirring constantly. Stir in mandarin segments and honey; cook 1 minute. Serve warm.

Makes about 1¾ cups sauce

❖

Cook's Tip

When measuring liquids, use a standard glass or clear plastic measuring cup. Place the cup on a level surface and fill to the desired amount. Bend down to read the marking; don't lift the cup off the surface to read. When measuring dry ingredients, use a measuring cup that's the exact capacity you wish to measure. Spoon the ingredient into the cup and level with the flat edge of a spatula.

❖

CHOCOLATE CAKE WITH ALMOND FROSTING

❖

Substituting puréed prunes for oil in this ultra-rich chocolate cake provides true low fat snacking.

❖

Nutrients per Serving:	
Calories	285
(2% of calories from fat)	
Total Fat	1 g
Saturated Fat	0 g
Cholesterol	0 mg
Sodium	274 mg
Carbohydrate	68 g
Dietary Fiber	1 g
Protein	5 g
Calcium	58 mg
Iron	3 mg
Vitamin A	13 RE
Vitamin C	1 mg

DIETARY EXCHANGES:
4 Starch/Bread

1 tablespoon instant coffee granules
1 cup boiling water
1 cup unsweetened cocoa powder
2 cups all-purpose flour
2 cups sugar
2 teaspoons baking soda
1 teaspoon baking powder
¼ teaspoon salt
1 cup skim milk
3 jars (2½ ounces each) puréed prunes
4 egg whites
1 tablespoon vanilla
½ teaspoon almond extract
  Almond Frosting (page 72)
¼ cup sliced toasted almonds (optional)

1 Preheat oven to 350°F. Spray 13×9×2-inch baking pan with nonstick cooking spray. Set aside.

2 Combine coffee granules and boiling water in measuring cup. Stir until coffee is completely dissolved. Set aside.

3 Sift cocoa into large bowl. Add flour, sugar, baking soda, baking powder and salt; mix well. In another large bowl, combine coffee, milk, prunes, egg whites, vanilla and almond extract; mix well. Add coffee mixture to cocoa mixture; mix well.

4 Pour batter into prepared pan. Bake 30 minutes or until wooden pick inserted in center of cake comes out clean. Cool in pan on wire rack 10 minutes. Invert onto serving plate; cool completely.

5 Prepare Almond Frosting; frost cake. Garnish with toasted almonds, if desired.

Makes 12 servings

(continued on page 72)

Chocolate Cake with Almond Frosting, continued

ALMOND FROSTING

   3 egg whites*
1½ cups firmly packed light brown sugar
 ¼ cup water
   1 teaspoon cream of tartar
   2 teaspoons vanilla
   1 teaspoon almond extract

1 Combine egg whites, brown sugar, water and cream of tartar in top of double boiler. Place over simmering water. Using electric hand mixer, beat until stiff peaks form, about 5 minutes.

2 Add vanilla and almond extract; beat 2 minutes. Remove from heat; cool.

*Use only clean, uncracked Grade A eggs.

❖

Cook's Tip
Baking a cake in a shiny aluminum, tin or stainless steel pan will result in a cake crust that will be lighter in color than one baked in a dull aluminum or tin pan.

❖

HAZELNUT BISCOTTI

These crunchy Italian cookies are traditionally served with a cup of hot cappuccino.

Nutrients per Serving:

(1 cookie)

|---|---|
Calories	76
(25% of calories from fat)	
Total Fat	2 g
Saturated Fat	<1 g
Cholesterol	0 mg
Sodium	50 mg
Carbohydrate	12 g
Dietary Fiber	<1 g
Protein	2 g
Calcium	6 mg
Iron	1 mg
Vitamin A	17 RE
Vitamin C	0 mg

DIETARY EXCHANGES:
1 Starch/Bread, ½ Fat

6 raw hazelnuts
2 tablespoons margarine
¼ cup sugar
2 egg whites, lightly beaten
1½ teaspoons vanilla
1½ cups all-purpose flour
½ teaspoon baking powder
⅛ teaspoon salt
½ teaspoon grated orange peel

1 Preheat oven to 375°F. Place hazelnuts in shallow baking pan; toast 7 to 8 minutes or until rich golden brown. Set aside. *Reduce oven temperature to 325°F.* Spray baking sheet with nonstick cooking spray. Set aside.

2 Combine margarine and sugar in medium bowl; mix well. Add egg whites and vanilla; mix well. Combine flour, baking powder, salt and orange peel in large bowl; mix well. Finely chop toasted hazelnuts; stir into flour mixture. Add egg white mixture to flour mixture; blend well.

3 Divide dough in half. Shape half of dough into log on lightly floured surface. (Dough will be fairly soft.) Repeat with remaining half of dough to form second log. Place logs on baking sheet. Bake both logs 25 minutes or until wooden pick inserted in centers of logs comes out clean. Cool on wire rack. *Reduce oven temperature to 300°F.*

4 When cool enough to handle, cut each log into 16 (½-inch) slices. Return slices to baking sheet. Bake slices 12 minutes. Turn slices over; bake additional 12 minutes or until golden brown on both sides. *Makes 16 servings*

OATMEAL ALMOND BALLS

¼ cup sliced almonds
⅓ cup honey
 2 egg whites
½ teaspoon ground cinnamon
⅛ teaspoon salt
1½ cups uncooked quick oats

1 Preheat oven to 350°F. Place almonds on cookie sheet; toast 8 to 10 minutes or until golden brown. Set aside. *Do not turn off oven.*

2 Combine honey, egg whites, cinnamon and salt in large bowl; mix well. Add oats and toasted almonds; mix well.

3 Drop by rounded teaspoonfuls onto ungreased nonstick cookie sheet. Bake 12 minutes or until lightly browned. Remove to wire rack to cool.   *Makes 24 servings*

Toasting almonds releases their full flavor and gives these cookies a rich, nutty taste.

Nutrients per Serving:
(1 cookie)

Calories	42
(19% of calories from fat)	
Total Fat	1 g
Saturated Fat	0 g
Cholesterol	0 mg
Sodium	16 mg
Carbohydrate	7 g
Dietary Fiber	0 g
Protein	1 g
Calcium	7 mg
Iron	0 mg
Vitamin A	0 RE
Vitamin C	0 mg

DIETARY EXCHANGES:
½ Starch/Bread

Cook's Tip
Store unopened packages of nuts in a cool dark place. Store opened packages in an airtight container in the refrigerator for six months or in the freezer for up to two years.

CARROT CAKE

❖

An average-size carrot has about 30 calories and contains enough beta-carotene to supply your body with more than 4 times the Recommended Dietary Allowance for vitamin A!

❖

Nutrients per Serving:

Calories	263
(18% of calories from fat)	
Total Fat	5 g
Saturated Fat	1 g
Cholesterol	15 mg
Sodium	274 mg
Carbohydrate	50 g
Dietary Fiber	1 g
Protein	4 g
Calcium	32 mg
Iron	1 mg
Vitamin A	422 RE
Vitamin C	3 mg

DIETARY EXCHANGES:
2½ Starch/Bread, ½ Fruit, 1 Fat

¼ cup walnuts, chopped
1 cup whole wheat flour
1 cup all-purpose flour
2 teaspoons baking soda
2 teaspoons ground cinnamon
½ teaspoon salt
1 whole egg
3 egg whites
1½ cups granulated sugar
¾ cup buttermilk
½ cup unsweetened applesauce
¼ cup vegetable oil
3 teaspoons vanilla, divided
2 cups grated, peeled carrots
1 can (8 ounces) crushed pineapple in juice, drained
1½ cups powdered sugar
1 tablespoon skim milk
1 tablespoon water

1 Preheat oven to 350°F. Spray 13×9×2-inch baking pan with nonstick cooking spray. Toast walnuts 8 to 10 minutes or until golden brown. Set aside. Do not turn off oven.

2 Sift both flours, baking soda, cinnamon and salt together in medium bowl; set aside. Lightly beat egg and egg whites in large bowl. Add granulated sugar, buttermilk, applesauce, oil and 2 teaspoons vanilla; mix well. Stir in flour mixture, carrots, pineapple and walnuts.

3 Pour batter into prepared pan. Bake 45 to 50 minutes or until wooden pick inserted in center comes out clean. Cool completely in pan on wire rack.

4 Combine powdered sugar, milk, water and remaining 1 teaspoon vanilla in medium bowl. Stir until smooth. Spread glaze over cooled cake. Garnish with additional chopped walnuts, if desired.

Makes 15 servings

PEANUT MERINGUE COOKIES

❖

*Create a virtually fat-free
snack by serving these
scrumptious meringue
cookies with fresh fruit.*

❖

Nutrients per Serving:

(1 cookie)

Calories	16
(15% of calories from fat)	
Total Fat	<1 g
Saturated Fat	0 g
Cholesterol	0 mg
Sodium	3 mg
Carbohydrate	3 g
Dietary Fiber	0 g
Protein	0 g
Calcium	1 mg
Iron	0 mg
Vitamin A	0 RE
Vitamin C	0 mg

DIETARY EXCHANGES:
½ Starch/Bread

4 egg whites
½ teaspoon cream of tartar
1 cup sugar
¼ cup ground peanuts

1 Preheat oven to 250°F. Line cookie sheet with parchment paper. Set aside.

2 Beat egg whites in large bowl with electric mixer until foamy. Add cream of tartar; beat until soft peaks form. Gradually add sugar; beat until stiff peaks form. Fold in peanuts.

3 Drop by teaspoonfuls onto prepared cookie sheet. Bake 20 minutes or until lightly browned. Cool on wire racks.

Makes 33 servings

❖

Cook's Tip
Store cooled meringue cookies in an airtight container at room temperature for two to three days. Freeze cookies in an airtight container for two weeks. Thaw, uncovered, at room temperature for 30 minutes.

❖

LEMON POPPY SEED CAKE

What a classic combination—lemon and poppy seed. Once you taste this luscious cake, you won't believe it's low fat!

❖

Nutrients per Serving:

Calories	217
(29% of calories from fat)	
Total Fat	7 g
Saturated Fat	1 g
Cholesterol	18 mg
Sodium	219 mg
Carbohydrate	34 g
Dietary Fiber	1 g
Protein	4 g
Calcium	69 mg
Iron	1 mg
Vitamin A	83 RE
Vitamin C	2 mg

DIETARY EXCHANGES:
2½ Starch/Bread, 1 Fat

6 tablespoons margarine, softened
½ cup firmly packed light brown sugar
½ cup plain low fat yogurt
1 whole egg
2 egg whites
3 teaspoons fresh lemon juice
1¾ cups all-purpose flour
1 teaspoon baking powder
½ teaspoon baking soda
¼ teaspoon salt
⅓ cup skim milk
2 tablespoons *plus* ½ teaspoon poppy seed
1 tablespoon grated lemon peel

1 Preheat oven to 350°F. Grease and flour 6-cup Bundt pan. Beat margarine in large bowl with electric mixer at medium speed until fluffy. Beat in brown sugar, yogurt, whole egg, egg whites and 3 teaspoons lemon juice. Set aside.

2 Combine flour, baking powder, baking soda and salt in medium bowl. Add flour mixture to margarine mixture alternately with milk, beginning and ending with flour mixture. Mix in 2 tablespoons poppy seed and lemon peel. Pour batter into prepared pan.

3 Bake about 40 minutes or until cake is golden brown and wooden pick inserted in center comes out clean. Cool in pan on wire rack 10 minutes; remove cake from pan and cool on wire rack. Prepare glaze; spoon glaze over cake and sprinkle with ½ teaspoon poppy seed. Garnish, if desired.   *Makes 12 servings*

LEMON GLAZE

1 cup powdered sugar
2½ tablespoons lemon juice

1 Mix powdered sugar with lemon juice until desired consistency.

MOCHA CRINKLES

Nutrients per Serving:

(1 cookie)

Calories	44
(30% of calories from fat)	
Total Fat	1 g
Saturated Fat	<1 g
Cholesterol	3 mg
Sodium	28 mg
Carbohydrate	7 g
Dietary Fiber	0 g
Protein	0 g
Calcium	7 mg
Iron	1 mg
Vitamin A	4 RE
Vitamin C	0 mg

DIETARY EXCHANGES:
½ Starch/Bread

1⅓ cups firmly packed light brown sugar
½ cup vegetable oil
¼ cup low fat sour cream
1 egg
1 teaspoon vanilla
1¾ cups all-purpose flour
¾ cup unsweetened cocoa powder
2 teaspoons instant espresso or coffee granules
1 teaspoon baking soda
¼ teaspoon salt
⅛ teaspoon ground black pepper
½ cup powdered sugar

1 Beat brown sugar and oil in medium bowl with electric mixer. Mix in sour cream, egg and vanilla. Set aside.

2 Mix flour, cocoa, espresso, baking soda, salt and pepper in another medium bowl.

3 Add flour mixture to brown sugar mixture; mix well. Refrigerate dough until firm, 3 to 4 hours.

4 Preheat oven to 350°F. Pour powdered sugar into shallow bowl. Set aside. Cut dough into 1-inch pieces; roll into balls. Roll balls in powdered sugar.

5 Bake on ungreased cookie sheets 10 to 12 minutes or until tops of cookies are firm to touch. (*Do not overbake.*) Cool on wire racks. *Makes 72 servings*

BERRY BUNDT CAKE

A cup of fresh, delicious blueberries or raspberries supplies about one-third of your daily vitamin C requirements. This fantastic berry cake contains 4 cups of berries!

2 cups all-purpose flour
1 tablespoon baking powder
1 teaspoon baking soda
¼ teaspoon salt
1 cup sugar
¼ cup vegetable oil
¾ cup buttermilk
½ cup cholesterol free egg substitute
2 cups frozen unsweetened raspberries
2 cups frozen unsweetened blueberries

1 Preheat oven to 350°F. Spray 6-cup Bundt pan with nonstick cooking spray. Set aside.

2 Combine flour, baking powder, baking soda and salt in large bowl. Combine sugar, oil, buttermilk and egg substitute in medium bowl. Add sugar mixture to flour mixture; stir just until moistened.

3 Fold in raspberries and blueberries. Pour batter into prepared pan. Bake 1 hour or until wooden pick inserted in center comes out clean. Cool in pan on wire rack. Serve with fresh berries, if desired.　　　　*Makes 12 servings*

Nutrients per Serving:

Calories	215
(21% of calories from fat)	
Total Fat	5 g
Saturated Fat	1 g
Cholesterol	1 mg
Sodium	262 mg
Carbohydrate	39 g
Dietary Fiber	2 g
Protein	4 g
Calcium	46 mg
Iron	1 mg
Vitamin A	58 RE
Vitamin C	6 mg

DIETARY EXCHANGES:
2 Starch/Bread, ½ Fruit,
1 Fat

Health Note
Originally, buttermilk was the name given to the residue left after butter was churned. Today, it is made by adding special bacterial cultures to low fat or skim milk, making it lower in fat and calories than even 2% milk.

WHOLE WHEAT OATMEAL COOKIES

❖

*Few things will produce a
smile as quickly as a plate
full of homemade
oatmeal cookies!*

❖

Nutrients per Serving:
(1 cookie)

Calories	55
(14% of calories from fat)	
Total Fat	1 g
Saturated Fat	0 g
Cholesterol	0 mg
Sodium	56 mg
Carbohydrate	11 g
Dietary Fiber	0 g
Protein	1 g
Calcium	10 mg
Iron	0 mg
Vitamin A	0 RE
Vitamin C	0 mg

DIETARY EXCHANGES:
1 Starch/Bread

1 cup whole wheat flour
1 teaspoon ground cinnamon
1 teaspoon baking powder
½ teaspoon baking soda
½ teaspoon salt
1 cup firmly packed light brown sugar
¼ cup unsweetened applesauce
2 egg whites
2 tablespoons margarine
1½ teaspoons vanilla
1⅓ cups uncooked quick oats
½ cup raisins

1 Preheat oven to 375°F. Lightly spray cookie sheets with nonstick cooking spray. Set aside.

2 Combine flour, cinnamon, baking powder, baking soda and salt in medium bowl; mix well.

3 Combine brown sugar, applesauce, egg whites, margarine and vanilla in large bowl. Mix until small crumbs form. Add flour mixture; mix well. Fold in oats and raisins.

4 Drop by rounded teaspoonfuls onto prepared cookie sheets, 2 inches apart. Bake 10 to 12 minutes or until golden brown. Cool on wire racks.

Makes 40 servings

PINEAPPLE-COCONUT UPSIDE-DOWN CAKE

❖

If you love the taste of piña colada, this extraordinary cake will not disappoint you!

❖

Nutrients per Serving:

Calories	272
(27% of calories from fat)	
Total Fat	8 g
Saturated Fat	2 g
Cholesterol	22 mg
Sodium	224 mg
Carbohydrate	47 g
Dietary Fiber	1 g
Protein	3 g
Calcium	57 mg
Iron	1 mg
Vitamin A	108 RE
Vitamin C	1 mg

DIETARY EXCHANGES:
3 Starch/Bread, 1½ Fat

2 tablespoons light corn syrup
6 tablespoons margarine, softened, divided
½ cup firmly packed light brown sugar
2 tablespoons flaked coconut
1 can (8 ounces) sliced pineapple in light syrup, drained
1⅓ cups all-purpose flour
2 teaspoons baking powder
¼ teaspoon salt
¾ cup granulated sugar
1 egg
1 teaspoon vanilla
⅔ cup skim milk
10 tablespoons light whipped topping

1 Heat corn syrup and 1 tablespoon margarine until melted in small skillet over medium heat. Stir in brown sugar; cook over medium heat until mixture is bubbly. Pour mixture into ungreased 9-inch round cake pan; sprinkle coconut evenly over top. Arrange whole pineapple slices on top of coconut.

2 Preheat oven to 350°F. Combine flour, baking powder and salt in medium bowl. Set aside. Beat remaining 5 tablespoons margarine in large bowl until fluffy; beat in granulated sugar, egg and vanilla. Add flour mixture to margarine mixture alternately with milk, beginning and ending with flour mixture. Pour batter into cake pan with prepared topping.

3 Bake about 40 minutes or until cake springs back when touched lightly. Cool in pan on wire rack 2 to 3 minutes; loosen side of cake with knife and invert onto serving plate. Cut cake into wedges. Serve warm or cool, topped with whipped topping. Garnish with pineapple slices, cherry and mint leaves, if desired.   *Makes 10 servings*

Personalized Nutrition Reference for Different Calorie Levels*

Daily Calorie Level	1,600	2,000	2,200	2,800
Total Fat	53 g	65 g	73 g	93 g
% of Calories from Fat	30%	30%	30%	30%
Saturated Fat	18 g	20 g	24 g	31 g
Carbohydrate	240 g	300 g	330 g	420 g
Protein	46 g**	50 g	55 g	70 g
Dietary Fiber	20 g***	25 g	25 g	32 g
Cholesterol	300 mg	300 mg	300 mg	300 mg
Sodium	2,400 mg	2,400 mg	2,400 mg	2,400 mg
Calcium	1,000 mg	1,000 mg	1,000 mg	1,000 mg
Iron	18 mg	18 mg	18 mg	18 mg
Vitamin A	1,000 RE	1,000 RE	1,000 RE	1,000 RE
Vitamin C	60 mg	60 mg	60 mg	60 mg

  * Numbers may be rounded
  ** 46 g is the minimum amount of protein recommended for all calorie levels below 1,800.
*** 20 g is the minimum amount of fiber recommended for all calorie levels below 2,000.

Note: These calorie levels may not apply to children or adolescents, who have varying calorie requirements. For specific advice concerning calorie levels, please consult a registered dietitian, qualified health professional or pediatrician.

VOLUME MEASUREMENTS (dry)

⅛ teaspoon = 0.5 mL
¼ teaspoon = 1 mL
½ teaspoon = 2 mL
¾ teaspoon = 4 mL
1 teaspoon = 5 mL
1 tablespoon = 15 mL
2 tablespoons = 30 mL
¼ cup = 60 mL
⅓ cup = 75 mL
½ cup = 125 mL
⅔ cup = 150 mL
¾ cup = 175 mL
1 cup = 250 mL
2 cups = 1 pint = 500 mL
3 cups = 750 mL
4 cups = 1 quart = 1 L

VOLUME MEASUREMENTS (fluid)

1 fluid ounce (2 tablespoons) = 30 mL
4 fluid ounces (½ cup) = 125 mL
8 fluid ounces (1 cup) = 250 mL
12 fluid ounces (1½ cups) = 375 mL
16 fluid ounces (2 cups) = 500 mL

WEIGHTS (mass)

½ ounce = 15 g
1 ounce = 30 g
3 ounces = 90 g
4 ounces = 120 g
8 ounces = 225 g
10 ounces = 285 g
12 ounces = 360 g
16 ounces = 1 pound = 450 g

DIMENSIONS

1/16 inch = 2 mm
⅛ inch = 3 mm
¼ inch = 6 mm
½ inch = 1.5 cm
¾ inch = 2 cm
1 inch = 2.5 cm

OVEN TEMPERATURES

250°F = 120°C
275°F = 140°C
300°F = 150°C
325°F = 160°C
350°F = 180°C
375°F = 190°C
400°F = 200°C
425°F = 220°C
450°F = 230°C

BAKING PAN SIZES

Utensil	Size in Inches/Quarts	Metric Volume	Size in Centimeters
Baking or	8×8×2	2 L	20×20×5
Cake Pan	9×9×2	2.5 L	22×22×5
(square or	12×8×2	3 L	30×20×5
rectangular)	13×9×2	3.5 L	33×23×5
Loaf Pan	8×4×3	1.5 L	20×10×7
	9×5×3	2 L	23×13×7
Round Layer	8×1½	1.2 L	20×4
Cake Pan	9×1½	1.5 L	23×4
Pie Plate	8×1¼	750 mL	20×3
	9×1¼	1 L	23×3
Baking Dish	1 quart	1 L	—
or Casserole	1½ quart	1.5 L	—
	2 quart	2 L	—